GROSS BUGS™

Stink Bugs

Jonathan Kravetz

The Rosen Publishing Group's
PowerKids Press™
New York

Published in 2006 by The Rosen Publishing Group, Inc.
29 East 21st Street, New York, NY 10010

First Edition

Editor: Jennifer Way
Book Design: Ginny Chu

Photo Credits: Cover and title page Clemson University - USDA Cooperative Extension Slide Series, www.insectimages.org; p. 5 Susan Ellis, www.insectimages.org; p. 6 © Gary W. Carter/Corbis; p. 9 Louis Tedders, USDA ARS, www.insectimages.org; p. 10 Robert L. Anderson, USDA Forest Service, www.insectimages.org; p. 13 Gary Bernon, USDA APHIS, www.insectimages.org; p. 13 (inset) Whitney Cranshaw, Colorado State University, www.insectimages.org; p. 14, 18 Russ Ottens, The University of Georgia, www.insectimages.org; p. 17 Susan Ellis, www.insectimages.org; p. 21 Jerry A. Payne, USDA ARS, www.insectimages.org.

Library of Congress Cataloging-in-Publication Data

Kravetz, Jonathan.
Stink bugs / Jonathan Kravetz.— 1st ed.
p. cm. — (Gross bugs)
Includes index.
ISBN 1-4042-3045-9 (lib. bdg.)
1. Stinkbugs—Juvenile literature. I. Title. II. Series: Kravetz, Jonathan. Gross bugs.

QL523.P5K73 2006
595.7'54—dc22
2004029382

Manufactured in the United States of America

CONTENTS

What Is That Smell?

Stink bugs got their name because they stink. When these colorful **insects** are in danger, they release a bad-smelling liquid from **glands** on their undersides. They even give off a smell when they die. The bad smells the bug gives off usually drive away enemies.

Stink bugs can be pests to farmers and gardeners. These bugs feed on many kinds of plants and vegetables. Stink bugs will often move from plant to plant while they eat. This means that each bug may harm several plants in a day. When there are many stink bugs doing this, they can cause a lot of harm to a garden or crop.

Stink bugs, like all insects, have six legs and **antennae**. Stink bugs belong to the Hemiptera **order**. This order also includes water bugs, bedbugs, and backswimmers.

This is a green stink bug. The stink bug's glands (*circled*) are where its bad smell comes from. Stink bugs belong to the Hemiptera, or "true bug," order. True bugs have mouthparts that allow them to suck juices from plants. Many true bugs are pests to farmers because of the harm they cause to plants.

These predatory stink bugs (*above*) are common in the southern United States. Predatory stink bugs are stink bugs that eat other insects. Farmers often consider them helpful because they eat pests that can harm crops. Brown and green stink bugs can live as far north as Quebec, Canada.

They Are Everywhere!

Although they are found all over the world, stink bugs are common in the United States. There may be stink bugs living in your backyard! Some common stink bugs in the United States are the green stink bug, the brown stink bug, and the harlequin stink bug.

In winter stink bugs enter a state called **diapause**. They can spend diapause under rotting leaves or tree bark. They sometimes try to get into houses to spend diapause. Once inside, stink bugs can leave behind their nasty odor on almost any surface they touch. The smell can last a long time.

GROSS FACT

Many people call any crawling thing a "bug." The insects in the Hemiptera order, however, are the only true bugs. The name Hemiptera means "half wings." The "half wings" are really the first pair of their two pairs of wings. The half of the wings near the base is tough, but it is thinner near the tips.

What a Stink Bug Looks Like

Stink bugs are easy to recognize because they have unusual wings. The front pair of wings is tough near the base and **membranous** toward the tips. That is why they are classified in the Hemiptera, or "half wing" order. All stink bugs have a shield shape. They also have a triangular bump on their **thorax**, called a scutellum.

Most stink bugs are around ½ inch (13 mm) long. Stink bugs come in many different colors. Some are brown. Others are gray or green. The different colors help the stink bug blend into its surroundings and avoid predators, or enemies. Some stink bugs have many bright colors, like red, orange, or yellow. These bugs taste very bad and their colors let birds know this.

This is a two-spotted stink bug. Adult stink bugs are strong fliers, which allows them to move easily among plants. The bright color of many stink bug species warns predators to stay away. If they do not, the predator could find itself eating a nasty-tasting meal!

A few species of stink bugs feed on other insects. Stink bugs that eat other insects use their mouthparts to poke a hole in and suck out the guts of the insect. This stink bug is eating a caterpillar.

What Stink Bugs Eat

Most stink bug **species** feed on plant sap. The southern green stink bug feeds on many types of fruit. It eats peaches and tomatoes, as well as seeds, such as pecans and soybeans. Stink bugs also feed on sap from wild plants. They suck the sap using their strawlike mouthparts. Some feed on many different plants, while others are pickier. Harlequin stink bugs eat plants in the broccoli family, such as cauliflower, brussels sprouts, and cabbage.

The stink bug's taste and smell keep them from being eaten by many predators. Stink bugs are hunted by many different animals, including birds, frogs, and lizards. These animals do not mind the smell and taste of the stink bug. Most animals, however, think twice about eating the stink bug because of the odor they can give off.

Stink Bug Eggs

Stink bugs undergo changes before becoming adults. Stink bugs go through three stages. These stages are egg, **nymph**, and adult. Their process of change is called an **incomplete metamorphosis**.

When first laid, the eggs of the green stink bug are yellow or green and shaped like tiny barrels. Soon they turn pink and then gray. Eggs of the green stink bug measure .06 by .05 inches (1.5 x 1.3 mm). The brown stink bug's eggs are white. They are a bit smaller than the eggs of the green stink bug. Southern stink bug eggs are cream colored and shaped like tubes. They turn pink before hatching. Stink bug eggs hatch in about one week, but they may take longer to hatch if the weather is colder.

These stink bug nymphs are at different nymphal states. The dark red nymph (*bottom center*) is the youngest. The light red nymph (*top right*) has just entered its second nymphal stage. The other nymphs are all further along in their second nymphal stage. *Inset:* This is a close-up view of stink bug eggs.

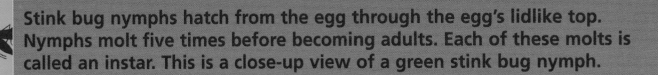

Stink bug nymphs hatch from the egg through the egg's lidlike top. Nymphs molt five times before becoming adults. Each of these molts is called an instar. This is a close-up view of a green stink bug nymph.

Young Bugs

After they hatch, young stink bugs are called nymphs. Nymphs look like small adults, but they do not have fully formed wings and they cannot **mate**. Stink bugs grow by **molting** their hard skin, or exoskeleton. Stink bug nymphs go through five molts, or instars, before molting a final time to become adults. Nymphs of the first stage do not eat.

Brown stink bug nymphs are yellow or tan with brown spots down the middle of their **abdomen**. Southern green stink bug nymphs are light green and have two rows of white spots on their back. Green stink bug nymphs are black when small, but as they grow they become green with orange and black markings. Depending on the species and the weather, it takes between 23 and 60 days for stink bugs to grow from an egg to an adult.

All Grown Up

When the nymphs are almost grown, they will move away from their mother. Once nymphs make their final instar, they are adults. They can fly and are able to mate. Adult stink bugs can live up to one year. The southern green stink bug lives from 65 to 70 days.

If a predator approaches, the stink bug will try to scare it off. The stink bug may wave its antennae or buzz its wings to frighten the attacker. If the attacker does not go away, the stink bug will give off its scent to chase it off. The stink bug's scent glands give off a sickening smell, and it spreads the odor as it flaps its wings. Making and giving off this chemical uses a lot of the stink bug's energy, so this is the bug's last choice when protecting itself.

This is an adult green stink bug. This type of stink bug feeds on crops such as cotton, peaches, and tomatoes. They can be found throughout North America.

In the late spring, adult stink bugs prepare to find a mate. Both male and female bugs give off pheromones from their abdomen in order to draw mates to them. Stink bugs of the opposite sex pick up this scent and approach a possible mate.

Mating

During winter adult stink bugs enter diapause. As the weather warms up in the spring, stink bugs come out of diapause and start feeding. The stink bugs will soon be strong enough to mate. Stink bugs use a chemical called a **pheromone** to draw members of the opposite sex to them. The pheromone is a different scent than the one they give off to scare off predators. Once they have found a partner, stink bugs mate by pressing their abdomens together. The male can then **fertilize** the female's eggs.

After mating female stink bugs begin laying their eggs. This is usually in early summer. They lay several hundred eggs in tight masses of around 30 eggs, mostly on the leaves of plants. Most stink bugs can produce offspring three times in a year.

Eating Crops

Many species of stink bugs feed on plants and can destroy important crops, such as peaches or tomatoes. Stink bugs poke their long mouthparts into fruit to feed. Their mouthparts leave holes in the fruit, and the holes cause the fruit to shrivel. This is often called catfacing. This makes the fruit look and taste bad. This means that farmers are not able to sell that crop. Stink bugs can cause millions of dollars' worth of harm in one year to just one crop.

Not all stink bugs harm crops. The Florida predatory stink bug is one of a few stink bugs that is considered a helpful insect. It eats other insect pests that harm plants, such as beetles and caterpillars.

This is a red harlequin stink bug. This bug attacks cauliflower and cabbage crops. Its mouthparts harm the plant, and the bad smell the bug leaves behind makes the plant unfit to eat.

How People Fight Stink Bugs

People attack crop-eating stink bugs with poisons that kill the bugs but do not harm crops. These poisons are called pesticides. When stink bugs get indoors, however, they can also cause problems for people. Stink bugs leave strong odors that can stay for six months or more. These odors draw other stink bugs. Even if all the stink bugs in a house are killed, the smell they leave behind will continue to draw new bugs.

The best way to keep stink bugs out of your house is to keep them from getting in. Sealing the cracks around windows, doors, pipes, and chimneys helps keep them out. Stink bugs are one of the smelliest animals on Earth and that is why they have continued to exist. No one wants to bother a creature that is so gross!

GLOSSARY

abdomen (AB-duh-min) The large, rear part of an insect's body.

antennae (an-TEH-nee) Thin, rodlike organs used to feel things, located on an animal's head.

diapause (DY-uh-pahz) A period when all growth is stopped.

fertilize (FUR-tuh-lyz) To put male cells inside an egg to make babies.

glands (GLANDZ) Organs or parts of the body that produce an element to help with a bodily function.

incomplete metamorphosis (in-kum-PLEET meh-tuh-MOR-fuh-sis) The series of changes that an insect undergoes when it changes from nymph to adult, resulting in an increase in size but not a great change in form.

insects (IN-sekts) Small creatures that often have six legs and wings.

mate (MAYT) To join together to make babies.

membranous (MEM-brayn-us) Having to do with a soft, thin layer of living matter that comes from a plant or an animal.

molting (MOHLT-ing) Shedding hair, feathers, shell, horns, or skin.

nymph (NIMF) A young insect that has not yet grown into an adult.

order (OR-dur) The scientific name for a very large group of plants or animals that are alike in some ways. It is a broader grouping than a family.

pheromone (FER-uh-mohn) A chemical produced by an animal that allows it to send a message to another of the same kind of animal.

species (SPEE-sheez) A single kind of living thing. All people are one species.

thorax (THOR-aks) The middle part of the body of an insect.

INDEX

Web Sites

Due to the changing nature of Internet links, PowerKids Press has developed an online list of Web sites related to the subject of this book. This site is updated regularly. Please use this link to access the list:
www.powerkidslinks.com/gbugs/stinkbugs/